In the Footsteps of my Forebears:
A Psychic's Journey Through Time

all my best

with

Beck

By William C. Becker

ISBN: ISBN-13: 978-0692948323
ISBN-10: 0692948325

Dedication

This book is dedicated to my grandparents, Maria and Alex Becker.

Acknowledgments

I want to give a special thank you to my sister, Susie Sumpter, for all of her help proof-reading and editing the book. I also want to thank Devin Conroy-Groves for all of the post work magic he did on my photos. Thank you to my cousin, Jim Card, for providing the photos I used on the cover. My Grandmother is holding my uncle William and my Grandfather is standing next to her in the front cover photo. The photo was taken when they landed at Philadelphia.

Introduction

In 1912, my grandparents left their village in the Volga German area of Russia to come to the United States. Our family is of German descent, but had lived in Russia since the 1760s when Catherine the Great brought in Germans to colonize the area around the Volga River.

My grandfather was a smart man. He could see the storm clouds of war gathering on the horizon as well as the building civil unrest in the country. He and Grandma decided to come to America with their infant son and wait out the coming storm. Then, when the Czar had everything back under control, they planned on returning to their villages and ancestral lands. We all know how well that worked out, so my grandparents stayed here.

I grew up with my grandmother talking about the old country, our family and the villages. All of my life I wanted to go visit the lands of my forebears, but it didn't seem like a dream that could possibly come true.

Then came the opportunity of a lifetime. A tour of the Volga German colonies was put together that included my grandparents' village. I jumped at the chance to go. I want to thank Dr. Brent Mai, Mila & Sergey Koretnikov, Elena Lozovaya, and Alexander Solovyev for making this life changing event happen.

I am a psychic medium. Part of what I wanted to do on this journey was to see what, if anything, I could pick up from my family and other Germans who had lived in these lands for 252 years. This book is about their journey and mine.

The First Colony

June 29th, 1764 is an important day in Volga German history. That's the day Dobrinka, the first Volga German colony, was settled.

Germans had been coming to Russia for some time before this. Peter the Great brought in German architects to build his new capital in St. Petersburg. Germans were brought in to run administrations, plan and even run the war machine at times. This case was a little different.

The areas further south along the Volga didn't have any permanent populations. Catherine the Great brought in the Germans to settle the land, farm and be a buffer against the nomadic tribes that would sometimes go through the area. My grandmother used to tell stories about the Kyrgyz and other nomadic peoples who had raided the villages at one time.

This monument was placed here to celebrate the 250th anniversary of the founding of the first Volga German settlement. While we were up here, I could see the dignitaries, the photographers and people dressed up dedicating the monument.

The main style of Church architecture in the Volga German area is called the Kontor Style, after the body that governed the Volga German area. There were four or six columns on each side. The front had a multistoried steeple and the bells were in a separate bell tower by the church. Men and women entered from opposite sides of the church and didn't sit together. When viewed from above, the plan is a cross. Catholic and protestant churches alike used this style except in the few cases where the village hired their own architects.

When I was standing in the front door of the church, I could see the people sitting in the pews – women on the left and men on the right. Solemn in many ways, some of the people (including women as not just men and children had to work at showing attention) were thinking of other things they needed, or wanted, to do.

Before 1933 all of the priests and pastors had been executed or sent to gulags. The churches were turned into "cultural centers" and the cemeteries of the Volga Germans had been destroyed. In his book, "The German-Russian Genocide: Remembrance in the 21st Century", Samuel D. Sinner states that the genocide started in the 1910s and continued through the 1940s. Sinner claims that from 1915 to 1945 mass executions, forced labor, sadistic starvation and vicious deportations claimed the lives of a million Russian Germans. The genocide continued during the reigns of Nicholas II, Lenin and Stalin. On August 28th 1941 Stalin published his resettlement decree. By the end of August/1st of September all Volga Germans had been transported to Siberia and Kazakhstan, leaving behind almost everything they owned.

The bricked in arch is where the door to the pulpit used to be. The area of older brick underneath it is where the pulpit actually was. It was here that the priest or minister would give his sermon during services. Standing in the midst of the ruins, I could see a man speaking. I can see him as I write this; not tall, grey hair, wire glasses, sad, harried... I get the feeling that this is either the end, or the beginning of the end for him and the congregation. I feel a sense of inevitability and knowledge of things to come and the sorrow of what has already come to pass.

The rectangular holes that run about half way up the wall show where the balcony that ran around most of the churches used to be.

The old original school building.

I didn't notice much at the time I took this photo, but now I see children at the lower floor windows. Younger kids with older ones behind them.

A group of men and women are walking down the street. They have hoes and rakes over their shoulders. It seems to be in earlier soviet times. They are worn down, but they do have some hope.

I can see a man and a woman in the yard. It looks like they are hoeing. The woman has a scarf on her head, long dress, the man has a hat, I don't know the name but would recognize the style. He's wearing long sleeves under suspenders. I see him both with and without a vest on. They both have dark colored clothes. Life is difficult. This appears to be a few years after the revolution.

One of the characteristics of this house that mark it as a German house is that there is a broad space between the top of the windows and the rafters. The Volga Germans put anywhere between a foot and a foot and a half of sod in that space for insulation. My grandmother said that they would use the attics as a place to hang the smoked meats and other things and then it would keep everything frozen during the winter, even though the house below was snug and warm.

Next Village

Unfortunately I can't quite get the name of this village from my notes and recordings.

The photo on the following page is a Catholic Church in another Village. The Kontor style of architecture was the one provided by the governing body for Lutheran and Catholic Churches. It's a style found only in the Volga German area. But colonies weren't limited to just that plan. If they had the resources, they could hire their own architects and build something to their own tastes. That's what this village did. And even the ruins are magnificent. This building is unique in that the crosses on the pinnacles are still in place. The Soviets took down most of the crosses in Russia.

Standing outside of this beautiful ruin I could see people walking down the streets on the way to church and other activities. They were wearing old fashioned clothes with the men often in long beards. Seeing these scenes takes me back to the time the people were alive. I can feel the emotions and basic attitude of the group.

Walking into this church was almost overpowering, there was such a strong sense of spirituality remaining.

The intricate window frames are still visible in some of the ruined churches and the birds love them.

The patterns in the brick work, along with the layers of plaster and paint, give an idea of the construction of the building. It was almost like being on an archeological dig!

I can see what looks like early teenage girls walking up these stairs, a type of bonnet on their heads.

One doesn't have to be psychic to be embraced by the awe and wonder in these ruins. The churches were the heart and soul of the villages. And all of that life has left a lasting impression. The people haven't gone. They left part of themselves here.

This was the schoolmaster's house. He would have been the most important man in the village after the minister or priest. But, as villages had traveling religious leaders that were only in town on occasion, the schoolmaster was the one person held in high esteem.

I could see the inhabitants of the house; proper, a bit stiff and formal.

Reinewald

The colony was founded on July 14, 1766, and was Lutheran. Every colony had craftsmen (blacksmith, tailor, etc.) but everyone had to farm as well. Mulberry trees and silk worms were introduced by a minister in that area and the colony became important for the manufacturing of silk.

Cossack Raiders would often attack and plunder the colonies. The raiders would also kidnap colonists and kill those that resisted. Many colonies built walls for protection, though we did not see any physical evidence of such town walls. The walls proved to provide only limited protection. The colonists then petitioned Catherine the Great to send troops. The presence of the troops mostly solved the issue. My grandmother would talk about the Cossack and Kyrgyz raiders and that they would steal children. She was born over a hundred years after the first settlements were founded, but the memory of the raids persisted.

This church was built in 1913. It is now a house of culture, so it remains mostly intact, although the steeple was removed. One of the things that continually amazes me is that so many grand churches were built between 1900 and 1914 and the start of WWI. Many built even in the last 2-3 years before the war. Life was prospering and evidently most people didn't see what was coming. No wonder my grandmother's family didn't believe Grandpa's predictions of the troubles to come, and refused to leave while they still could. She had an aunt on her mother's side here, and very few other relatives, even distant ones. Grandpa had cousins over here and a brother in Colorado already by 1912 when my grandparents made the journey.

Inside the old church/active cultural center
(Additional photos on the following pages.)

It was interesting seeing the inside of the building. I could sense the history and depth of the activity in what had been the sanctuary. I could feel the church services, as well as see the later days of dances, movies and yes, indoctrination rallies and lectures! The center also has a small museum area. Some of the items are from the German days, some the Soviet, and some showcasing what is happening in the village today (photos below). The feel of this as a central meeting place in the past is strong. It still is, but doesn't feel as important in some ways now. I think because of the other forms of activity available.

The schoolmaster's house

The Schoolmaster was the 2nd most important person in town, after the priest or minister. As most villages didn't have their own ministers, the schoolmaster officiated at deaths and baptisms. He would lead the Sunday services and basically step in for the minister in most ways. Weddings would usually wait until the actual minister was in town, so there could be several weddings at once or in a day.

The old school that is still used as a school

Stahl

One of the big problems in colonies was fire. In many villages, each house had a picture of what they needed to bring with them to fight fires in the villages. Some houses had pictures of buckets, some had ladders, others axes or hammers, and so on.

In 1921 the revolt of hungry peasants started here and their headquarters were in this village. Men from other colonies were called in to be part of the rebellion. If they didn't show up and participate, they could be shot. A few months later the Red Army came in and shot the rebels. The colony started a deeper collapse during this time.

This is the site of the old Volga German cemetery. The headstones and all mention of the cemetery were destroyed and erased. The bodies were left. This is very common in the old Volga German villages. It was part of the genocide against my people. I see men digging, they feel like grave diggers. They are wearing dark clothes, jackets and trousers, there is a sadness and sense of loss. I can see entities wandering and looking down as they walk. They are not spirits, but part of the energy that was created by the shock and horror of the attempts to wipe all memory of us out. They are wandering as though they are looking for something; some for their graves, some for the graves of loved ones. It is important to know, though, that the souls are not trapped here.

Rosenheim

The village was founded in 1765. In 1914 a Russian name was given to it because of anti-German sentiments. In 1918, with the creation of the Volga German Commune, it got its German name back.

Catholic Church Ruins – I can see a service going on. Sense of the people coming up to the communion rail. Later years, as the house of culture, I can see them dancing. People watching movies, propaganda. People in the balcony looking down, dressed in their finest clothes. Very beautiful.

There is a peasant woman with scythe outside the door. Seeing this as I stood in the ruins looking out was very surprising at first. She was so close it seemed odd that there would be agricultural grasses growing so close to the church. But then it was explained (I think by her) that nothing, including land, was wasted. I think this was after the revolution.

The Communion rail was here. I see people kneeling as they receive Communion.

Enders

Enders was founded in 1765 and was a Lutheran colony. There aren't many Volga German houses left, and most of the remaining houses are used as dachas.

This is a good example of a Volga German house. There aren't any doors on the street, only windows. The foundation is stone. The house is then built like a log cabin, although here they wrap the ends of the wood. The eves of the roof line are very high above the windows, leaving a space for 12-18 inches of sod for insulation. In Russian houses the eves come down to the tops of the windows. Most have beautiful windows and shutters. Small brick houses are often actually wooden, with a brick overlay.

I think the old cemetery was in the field behind the playground. I saw many people rising up from the ground, they were obviously dead. It reminded me of the dream sequence from Fiddler on the Roof! They kept coming and were not happy. I could tell things weren't set right. They were very angry. Not really at the current people so much as those who had killed them and desecrated the cemetery.

I could also see someone hanging in the trees you see in the above photo. This seems like a mob type execution and goes back to the times of the genocide or just before. He's on the viewer's right.

Marx

This Lutheran church is being restored. It was the largest on that side of the Volga and considered the Lutheran Cathedral on that side of the river.

This building was part of a series in a school that we went to for a
toilette stop as well as visiting the village. I saw a man with a rifle at
the doorway. My first thought was that he was a custodian, but he
had the rifle. With the strife and violence that happened in the
area after the revolution, it's possible.

Zurich

This church was never completely destroyed, and is being renovated.

I could see the priest at the altar and people sitting. This was the first place we visited that really had a sense and feel of spirituality.

When I went up to the balcony, I could see people gathered for events and also watching performances. That stemmed from the Soviet period when it was used as a house of culture. I could also see marriages. The bride seemed to be in white. Grandma's wedding dress was green.

This is the old school building. During the Spanish Civil War, this was used as an orphanage for children from Spain. The Soviets supported Franco. The building has an air of sadness and feels forlorn. I can still sense children in the windows, looking out, waiting for someone to take them home, waiting for their parents. This is strongest from the upper floor.

I also saw a group of people walking with their few possessions down the street. They looked lost and confused, not knowing where they were going and why. I think this might have been before the mass deportation of 1941. The time period for the clothes looks earlier. But I could be wrong. It's possible that with the poverty and insecurity after the revolution, the periods of violence and genocide and famine, that styles didn't change much and people weren't getting new clothes very often.

Mariental

I can see Mass being said, the priest is elevating the consecrated host.

The church burned in 2001. Everyone was upset except one man who was happy and full of joy and clapping his hands as it burned. The people asked him why? Then, a few years later, his house caught fire. The fire killed him, his mother and his grandson. So the villagers said, "See, this is what happens when you sin." They tell the story to all visitors.

This is also the Catholic church where in 1932 all of the priests gathered together and said Mass before being sent to the gulags.

These hills were called the Kyrgyz hills by the colonists. It was from over these hills that the nomadic raiders would storm the colony. There are many German tales of the raiders coming and stealing everything, even taking people. My grandmother used to talk about the Kyrgyz coming and stealing children. That wasn't happening in her time, I don't think, but the stories and fear were fresh.

I can see the raiders, on camel- and horseback, riding over the hills. Swords raised, long guns waiving. Fearsome men intent on plunder and terror! Catherine the Great eventually sent Cossacks to protect the colonies which eventually stopped the raids.

This is the monument to the 250th anniversary of the founding of the colony.

This area is where the old German cemetery and chapel used to be. I can see people in their best clothes, looking down. I can also see the dead that were buried there. White faced, sad and angry, and unhappy. One man in particular is very irate. This was part of the genocide of the Germans. We were to be erased.

This shows the location better. The foundations were part of the chapel.

Dehler

The church had been here. A deep, deep sadness, a universal sadness - Universal collective cry in silence about the inhumanity. The soul destruction, the destruction of spirit, not just the body, the destruction of humanity on a cosmic level. That is part of what genocide does. And this is part of what I feel in all of the locations. It's more than that – a deep mourning for humanity.

Bangert

This is a village that was moved as the river was dammed in 1961. So while the sadness is there it is much less pronounced. There is more of a feeling of hard work and a feel of sadness from being so controlled.

I see an old couple in this house. They are sitting down for a meal of porridge, rough furniture – hand made. They seem to be dressed in clothes from the 1800s. The year 1835 pops into my mind. They don't have much money. The porridge is their dinner. They are sad. The younger ones have gone away. It's not clear if they went to the city or out of the country, but I picked up South America – Argentina in particular.

Stahl... the other Stahl

The village was moved when the dam was built, flooding it. The humps that can be seen by the river are all foundations from buildings.

This isn't our village, but it was a beautiful spot for a family photo. I'm with the cousins I took the tour with. I love the way this tiny out cropping is set up! I look like the tallest of the group! In reality, Harlen is the tallest.

In the front row from left to right: Caren Springer, Carolyn Camp, Bob Card
Back row from left to right: Harlen Springer, Jim Card, Tari Card, and William Becker

This is one of the only Volga German tombstones still intact. The legend is, some people thought they would bring in a crane to take the stone and sell it or use it for some other purpose; many of the headstones were used in new buildings. But it seems that someone or something was protecting the stone. As the robbers were attempting to steal the stone, the crane broke and killed one of the men. That is why the stone was allowed to remain in its proper place.

This was a parochial school then, later, a house of culture. I could see a couple of children looking out of the second window. One kid was older, one younger. Then more and more came until several where looking to see what was going on! Someone else was looking out of the first window. I'm not sure who.

There was also someone looking out of the boarded up window of the school masters house next door. It was the school master. He was upset – who were these people disrupting his school? Why were they there? How dare they be there without asking his permission! Partly he was concerned about the safety of the children. Mostly he was concerned about his authority and that he hadn't been consulted. He has a very fragile ego.

Not far from this spot was where the church had been. I could see the minister walking down the aisle, incense burner swinging. He seems to be walking in the direction of the river. Unfortunately, it seems that I didn't take a photo of the spot!

This plane is one that was used to train pilots. I can see 2 pilots in the plane. Yuri Gagarin, the first man in space, used this particular plane to learn to fly. This fascinating museum is in Saratov.

Warenburg

The colony was founded in 1767. The church shown on the
following pages was built in 1910. During the Soviet era, the cross
was taken down and replaced by a red star. The legend is that soon
after, family members of those who replaced the cross started
getting sick and dying. After 2000, someone paid to have the star
taken down. And the deaths stopped!

I can see people coming in. A certain amount of prestige. A lighter, happier feel here going back to the time of the Millers, who were

benefactors. It seems like life was a little better, a little richer, here than other places. A sadness now that all of that is gone. Dark and the drab and oppressed and the anguish of souls. Also a layer of the hard work, labor and toil of the daily life of the people. And a joy and celebration and excitement for life, a big party in a sense that was a deeper meaning of joy. One of the joys and challenges of reading places of history is that I usually pick up on many different layers of history and people. Sometimes it's clear where the lines between them are. At other times they tend to blend together a bit. Personally, I love it all. This ability makes travel so much more enriching and enjoyable for me.

I could see someone hanging from this beam. It looked like a minister or pastor, and felt like this happened during the 1920s. I don't have verification of this but with the genocide, even if the minister was living here until 1933, by then all of them were assassinated or in gulags. I don't know if he hung himself, or was lynched, but it feels like a lynching by peasants. This could have been during the famine of the 1920s.

Warenburg Cemetery – I got some similar imagines to those in some of the other cemeteries; older men, some with long grey beards, dark hats. Some had mustaches like grandpa had when they came over. "Why are we here? Why are you here?" Stern and watchful. An underlying peace; fairly typical in the few cemeteries we'd gone to.

This is the oldest part of the old German cemetery. A few headstones remain that were either too big to move or weren't wanted.

The indents and mounds are the tombs. The bodies were buried in underground vaults.
I felt a spirit of "gone away" – gone with the wind, so to speak. And I saw vague, shadowy figures all over, watching.

The graves here were in underground vaults.

Seelmann

This colony was founded in 1767.

I see an old, skinny guy looking out the boarded up window at us.
He is short and bald, with a long white beard. He has an old woman
with a headscarf with him. She is short and squat.

People are looking out of the first window by the sign. Mostly they are children. A younger man and woman peeking out the window are afraid of getting caught at something.

The relief effort for the colonies on this side of the river, including Brunnental, was centered here.

Some of the villages now have museums in them. In the past, the German influence and habitation of the lands had been ignored, but now the whole history is coming more to light in these places. This photo and the one on the previous page are from the museum in this village.

Looking at the clocks, I see a clock maker or jeweler working on them. He has a glass and is examining the works, working on the mechanism, working on the gears. It's quite lovely. Then I see the same kind of man, he did build at least some of the clocks, as he works on them, adjusting them, treating them kindly like a fine work of art.

The man in this portrait looks very similar to the gentleman I saw with the clocks. Could be him but I'm not sure.

Brunnental

Finally, we have arrived in the village that was impetus for me taking this tour. We have reached the village in which my grandparents grew up and were married. This was the village they left in 1912 to build up resources, but mostly to allow the Czar to regain control of a country that was spiraling out of control. My grandfather was smart. He could see the handwriting on the wall, and he'd served in the Czar's army before. He wasn't going to do so again! We all know how well the Czar did regaining control and stability in Russia. My grandparents never did go back. They did write back and forth during periods when it was allowed. They also sent blankets, money, clothing, and whatever else they could to family members during the periods that it was permitted by the government.

I remember while I was growing up that Grandma would occasionally get a letter from one of her sisters, or hear from someone else about how the few family members that survived were doing. We sometimes sent photos, but we had to be very careful not to dress too well, show too much affluence or even the sign of too much food on the table. Letters were heavily censored and anything showing a much better life over here could be cut out or simply not delivered. This was in the 1960s and 70s! During the best of times under the Soviet Union one could never guarantee that mail would arrive. It's interesting, Grandma had the same thought that most people did in the Russian literature and history I've read: "If the Czar only knew." People tended to think that if the Czar had been aware of the problems they faced, he would have taken care of the issues and protected his people.

We were met by a huge flock of crows when we entered the village. This photo doesn't do justice to the number of them. It looked like there were thousands of swarming black birds. They stayed with us – my cousins and me particularly – until we were at the site of Grandma's house, then they left! The crows returned as we were getting ready to leave the village. This day was one of firsts! And the experience with the crows was one of those!

Brunnental was a daughter colony of Frank, Kolbe, and Walter and founded in 1855. In 1910 the population was 4,600. Grandma's father was the head of the administration for the area, and was in charge of taking that census. Grandma assisted him.

The Lutheran church was built in 1877. As was typical of the German churches, the church bells came from Germany. They had disappeared for some time, but the smallest one has been found and located at the city hall – which had been the house of one of Grandma's cousins, Heinrich Hart.

The school was built in 1895. Grandma went to school in this building. And I had a very heartfelt and wonderful conversation with her here. I'll talk more about it later.

These are photos of Grandma's paternal grandfather's house. Grandma seemed to have a very close relationship with him. She said that he was the richest man in town, if not the area. I know that he had a large number of both horses and camels. And, in a time and place where most people's wealth consisted of their land and livestock, he actually had a great deal of cash! Surprisingly, I didn't really pick up much at this location.

These photos are of where Grandma's father's house used to stand. It was still standing in the 1980's but the neighbor said it had fallen into disrepair and was knocked down in 1997.

I got a sense of people in the house with a great deal of sadness. A woman putting things away for the last time – packing little bits, but I don't see baggage. I saw my great-grandfather and great-grandmother before a chest or bureau or desk type piece of furniture. They kept opening a drawer, taking out something – papers I think, then putting them back. Like they were putting things away for the last time, wanting to leave the house in good order. Maybe they thought that they would come back, but what I picked up was that they knew they were leaving never to return. They were confused, heartbroken really. They seemed without hope; not understanding why this was happening to them. They had suffered so much for so long already. It was a heart wrenching scene. I also felt there was a sense of knowing they should have come over here with Grandma and Grandpa.

This is the store Grandma's cousin or uncle owned. I've heard both versions of the story!

I'm standing in front of Grandpa's father's house. (Lower photo of previous page.) It certainly isn't in the shape it would have been when my great-grandfather owned it!

This spot was entertaining. Grandma had told me all sorts of stories about Grandpa's evil stepmother. Dad also told me stories he'd heard. When Grandpa came back from serving a term in the Czar's army, his stepmother wouldn't give him enough to eat. He had to steal food in his own father's house! Also, when they were getting ready to come over to the U.S., my grandparents stayed here. The wicked stepmother had Grandma slopping the hogs and doing all sorts of heavy work while she was very pregnant. The stepmother also stole from my grandparents.

So, when I got here, the stepmother came flying (literally) out of the top part of the house, yelling and nattering at me! She didn't like me one bit! She also didn't like the condition of her house! She knew that I knew her nasty secrets and what a horrible person she had been. I laughed at her, which made her even angrier. She couldn't intimidate me. She knew I knew she had no power over me. I'm keeping the conversation with and about her to the G-rated version! Some of my cousins got to hear a bit more!

I also did see my great-grandfather. He would be yelling back and forth with her, then he would be brow beaten and back away. What a toxic and hard life he lived with her.

I'd wanted to tell that evil troll off all of my life, and I got the chance to! I guess this was a trip in a lifetime in more ways than I first thought!

The cousins In front of grandpa's house.

This is Grandpa's father's brother's house. It's just across the street.

This is Grandma's maternal grandfather's house. I didn't get anything from it.

The photo on the previous page is one of the stairways in the school. I started by seeing school children coming down the stairs. Then I saw Grandma as a young girl coming down the stairs! She waved as a young girl and also showed me herself as I knew her. She was glad that we came. She is happy and thriving. She said that it doesn't matter that her father's house is gone. And she's now laughing about Grandpa's stepmother. She can't hurt her or anyone now. Grandma is actually somewhat sympathetic in that she felt a bit sorry for the stepmother because she had always been very unhappy – she had an unhappy life.

This is the new cemetery. None of my people are buried here. They are probably in the field over. But as we were here and getting ready to leave Brunnental, Grandma was smiling down and waving, both as the young girl, and as I knew her.

The crows gathered again as we were leaving the cemetery. Then we were treated to this glorious sunset as we headed on our way out of town. I'll remember this day the rest of my life!

Addendum

Stalingrad

The following photos are from the Battle of Stalingrad Museum (where the incredible diorama of the battle is housed) and from the Stalingrad Memorial. I've included these locations for a few reasons. One, the scope of the destruction and loss of life is beyond the imagination. WWII did affect the Germans that still managed to live in the Soviet Union in that the final expulsion and exile (for those that survived the expulsion) of the Germans was triggered by Hitler's invasion. And, in a sense of irony, the building left standing (shown on next page) to show the extent of some of the damage, was a German factory, and one of the only buildings to survive the battle intact was a large German house!

The soldiers inside the factory became clear to me. I could see the shooting back and forth, I could see the bombs. I saw and felt the horror.

I could also see factory workers here. And I could see them making something having to do with armaments.

The area is haunted, as one might expect. The round, light colored building behind the ruined factory houses the museum and diorama of the battle. In one area, I could sense a deep heaviness. It was actually hard to walk for a minute. I saw soldiers fighting. I saw soldiers dying and fatigued. In one spot I saw a soldier as he was shot and died. I couldn't tell which side he was on.

There were soldiers standing in shock and total horror. The inhumanity is beyond comprehension.

This statue (previous page) is on top of the memorial hill. Under the statue are the bodies of at least 30,000 fallen soldiers who were defending Stalingrad from the German invasion.

Epilog

I took this journey through time to bring myself closer to my family history and the lives my grandparents lived in the "Old Country". I grew up with the stories my grandmother told of life in her family in Czarist Russia and their journey here. I wanted to walk in the footsteps of my ancestors and see the places in which they lived. I did all of this and more.

My travels not only brought my family history closer to me, but also showed me more of the real life in the Volga German colonies both before and after the 1917 revolution and WWII. I was able to grasp that there was a real genocide against my people that lasted through many years. I saw the discrimination my people suffered, just because they were of German descent. And, I saw more of the aftermath of war on the people. The experience was one of joy, and sorrow, and an even stronger resolve to work for peace between peoples and the elimination of prejudice.

Not only do I want to thank the people who made this remarkable experience of a lifetime happen for me, but I also want to express my appreciation and love to my grandparents and all of the family members and others in the realm of the "breathing impaired" that talked to me and let me get a glimpse of their lives and stories.

Made in the USA
Lexington, KY
04 April 2018